MARTIN LEMAN'S

Teddy Bears

First published in Great Britain in 1996 by Brockhampton Press,
a member of the Hodder Headline Group, 20 Bloomsbury Street, London WC1B 3QA.

This series of little gift books was made by Frances Banfield, Kate Brown, Laurel Clark,
Penny Clarke, Clive Collins, Melanie Cumming, Nick Diggory, Deborah Gill, David Goodman,
Douglas Hall, Maureen Hill, Nick Hutchison, John Hybert, Kate Hybert, Douglas Ingram,
Simon London, Patrick McCreeth, Morse Modaberi, Tara Neill, Anne Newman, Grant Oliver,
Michelle Rogers, Nigel Soper, Karen Sullivan and Nick Wells.

ISBN 1 86019 467 2
A copy of the CIP data is available from the British Library upon request.

Produced for Brockhampton Press by Flame Tree Publishing,
a part of The Foundry Creative Media Company Limited,
The Long House, Antrobus Road, Chiswick W4 5HY

Printed and bound in Italy by L.E.G.O. Spa.

CELEBRATION

MARTIN LEMAN'S

Teddy Bears

Selected by Karen Sullivan

Love me, love my Teddy Bear.

Anonymous

Books were my first friends; for a long time my only friends, apart from a teddy bear called Onjie ...

Bernard Levin, *Enthusiasms*

A bear, however hard he tries,
Grows tubby without exercise. ...
He's proud of being short and stout.

A. A. Milne, *Teddy Bear*

There is no need to tell you how special a teddy bear is ...

Anonymous

Cuddly and warm, these calming creatures reassure me in the days when fears fly before reason and the world looms bleak instead of beautiful. The Teddy Bear, all things to all ages ... symbol that all is right with the world if only one believes.

Anonymous

I am a bear of Very Little Brain, and long words Bother me.

A. A. Milne, *Winnie-the-Pooh*

You need a bear to get you through the measles. Especially when you're supposed to have grown up.

Clara Ortega

2

When I ask Daddy
Daddy says ask Mummy.
When I ask Mummy
Mummy says ask Daddy.
I don't know where to go.

Better ask my teddy
He never says no.

John Agard,
Ask Mummy Ask Daddy

Oh yes. Don't you remember last term when I took Aloysius and left him behind I didn't know where. I prayed like mad to St Anthony of Padua that morning, and immediately after lunch there was Mr Nichols at Canterbury Gate with Aloysius in his arms, saying I'd left him in his cab.

Evelyn Waugh, *Brideshead Revisited*

There was an Old Person of Ware
Who rode on the back of a bear,
When they ask'd 'Does it trot?'
He said, 'Certainly not!
He's a Moppsikon, Floppiskon Bear!'

Edward Lear

One of a teddy's best qualities is that he can listen without judging.

Anonymous

Teddy it seems is man enough to inspire jealousy as well as love.

Anna Baranski

I heard the church bells hollowing out the sky,
Deep beyond deep, like never-ending stars,
And turned to Archibald, my safe old bear,
Whose woollen eyes looked sad or glad at me,
Whose ample forehead I could wet with tears,
Whose half-moon ears received my confidence,
Who made me laugh, who never let me down.

John Betjeman, *Summoned by Bells*

Bears make life more bearable. They are remarkable company when one is alone.

Nesta Wyn Ellis

'Pooh,' said Christopher Robin earnestly, 'If I ... If I'm not quite –'
he stopped and tried again – 'Pooh, whatever happens, you will
understand, won't you?'

A.A. Milne, *Winnie-the-Pooh*

Dolls may come and dolls may go, but somehow Teddies go on for ever.

Michael Bond, *Book of Bears*

Wonderful bears that walked my room all night,
Where are you gone, your sleek and fairy fur.
Your eyes veiled imperious light?

Adrienne Cecile Rich

Dolly is lying in the closet,
Since my brown bear came,
He is shaggy, big and woolly,
Teddy is his name.

Anonymous

His quizzical, faintly melancholy face sympathised with my myriad
woes. I wept into his golden fur, pillowed my head on his comfortable
stomach and did my homework under his benevolent eye.

Mrs James Dow McCallum

Anybody who takes me must take my bears or stay out of my life.

Anonymous

I love my little Teddy Bear
He's such a friendly fellow
His fur beautiful and soft,
Is neither brown nor yellow ...
He's such a quiet little chap
He never barks, he has no fleas,
At least he never scratches.

Mrs Eulia Smith Zimmerman

What a miracle life is, and how whimsical that in all their wonder and their pain, their confusion and their joy, human beings had the idea to create teddy bears to keep them company and help them make it through the hard times.

Ted Menton

Fuzzy Wuzzy was a bear
Fuzzy Wuzzy had no hair
Fuzzy Wuzzy wasn't very fuzzy
Wuz he?

Traditional

People in all walks of life love Teddy Bears. Some of the most famous people in the world today still cherish their faithful old friends from childhood – just as do uncounted thousands of ordinary men and women. Indeed, it makes no difference whether you're rich or poor, distinguished or just plain average; teddy can have precisely the same effect on you. And it's something no one need be the slightest bit embarrassed about.

Philippa and Peter Waring, *The Teddy Bear Lovers' Book*

If was the perfect tree house ... Pooh and I claimed it. It was Pooh's house really, but there was plenty of room for us both inside, and here we came to play our small, quiet, happy games together.

Christopher Milne, *The Enchanted Places*

Punny Bear
What do you call a Teddy Bear fib?
Why, a bear-faced lie of course.

Teddies go everywhere and do everything. They are part of our everyday lives.

Margaret Hutchings

The king just laughed as the train pulled out,
But he said to himself as he turned about,
'It would help me carry my country's cares,
If every home had teddy bears.'

Seymour Eaton

Teddy, Teddy, you're my sweetheart true.
You're never bold
You never scold
You all my troubles share.
What would I do without you dear
Old Teddy Teddy Bear.

Traditional rhyme

One bear at bedtime is all I need.

Mick Inkpen, *One Bear at Bedtime*

It is the charm of bears that they cannot be bored.

Anonymous

Monday's bear is fair of face.
Tuesday's bear is full of grace.
Wednesday's bear is full of woe.
Thursday's bear has far to go.
Friday's bear is loving and giving.
Saturday's bear works hard for a living.
But the bear born on the Sabbath day,
Is happy and wise and good and gay.

Ted Menton, *The Bear Lovers' Catalogue*

'Help,' said Eddy. 'I'm scared already!
I want my bed! I want my teddy!'

Jez Alborough, *Where's My Teddy?*

Someone soft and warm
Someone quiet and understanding,
Always willing to listen
Always willing to play,
Anytime of the day
Always there,
Teddy Bear.

Judith Robins

During the fifteen years or so in which I have been connected with the
dear creatures I have met many fascinating, warm and totally sane
people. I can't remember meeting anyone interested in the phenomenon
of the Teddy who was bitter, unpleasant or downright beastly.

Peter Bull, *A Hug of Teddy Bears*

A cheerful old bear at the zoo
Could always find something to do.
When it bored him to go
On a walk to and fro,
He reversed it, and walked fro and to.

Traditional

Any Teddy Bear who
is at all important
should be hugged
immediately.

Ted Menton

A stitch in time saves nine ...
but a stitch in a bear saves stuffing.

Anonymous

So they went off together. But wherever they go, and whatever happens to them on the way, in that elevated place on top of the Forest a little boy and his Bear will always be playing.

A.A. Milne, *The House at Pooh Corner*

If you have a Teddy Bear I don't see how you could ever get rid of it. After all, there's no scheme for pensioning off old Teddy Bears.

Clement Freud

My teddy bear is quite old. My auntie had it. It has one eye and the other has fallen off.

Bella, 6

Teddies spell comfort and security. They remind grown-ups of the happiest times of their childhood. There's nothing threatening about him – he never yells back! And it's comforting to have something around that's lived with you all your life. And still likes you.

Dr Leonard Kristal

I take my teddy very seriously. I've met human beings who didn't have half the personality he has.

Noele Gordon

Teddy Bears are so much cheaper than a psychiatrist and not nearly so supercilious.

Peter Bull

Two terrible tubby teddies, taking treacle tea together,
Turned topsy-turvy tricycle tricks,
Trying to toast ten tiddlywinks.

Jean Greenhouse, *Teddy Tongue Twister*

Even though there is a rip in your teddy bear, the love will not fall out.

Eve Frances Gigliotti and Elaine Claire Gigliotti

Teddy be nimble,
Teddy be quick,
Teddy jump over
The candlestick.

Traditional

The black bear's name was Teddy-B;
The B for black or brown you see.
And Teddy G was the gray bear's name;
The G for gray; but both bears came
For 'Teddy' because everywhere
Children called them Teddy Bears.

The 'Teddy' part is the name they found,
On hat and tree and leggin's round,
On belt and boot and plates of tin,
And scraps of paper and biscuits thin,
And other things a hunter dropped
At a mountain camp where he had stopped.

And how some boys, the stories tell
Liked these two Teddy Bears so well
That they made a million for the stores to sell,
Some quite little for children small,
And some as big as the bears are tall;
The brown ones looking like Teddy-B
And the white as funny as Teddy-G.

Seymour Eaton, *The Travelling Bears*

33

Despite broken growls, noses hanging by the slenderest of threads, worn paws, and the occasional loss of an eye, they remain steadfast and true through thick and thin. They are there when wanted, but quite content to await your pleasure ... an ideal recipe for the perfect friendship.

Michael Bond

My Teddy Bear was the very first masculine love in my life.

Barbara Cartland

The mystique lies in the faces of the bears themselves.

Peter Bull

Dear Mr Mitchom,
I don't think my name is likely to be worth much in the toy bear business but you are welcome to use it.

Letter from Theodore 'Teddy' Roosevelt to Morris Mitchom,
maker of the first official Teddy Bears, 1903

The Teddy Bear has been a success with all ages since his very first appearance. All this summer he has been seen at the most fashionable resorts, often displaying a wardrobe fit for a leader of fashion. To say that the Teddy Bear has put the nose of the doll out of joint is really to express it mildly. The funny bear is hugged and loved by more little people in this land then you can count. And as a Christmas present he is showing every sign of being unrivalled ...

Woman's Home Companion magazine, 1912

Englishmen are far more ready than Americans to confess that they hang onto their bears. ... Over there they tend to think that any such sentimentality is a reflection on their virility.

Peter Bull

The cult of the Teddy Bear now has the status of something like a fringe religion. Sometimes 15,000 and more bear enthusiasts turn up at picnics to swop stories about their bears and show them off. Mrs Thatcher, for instance, has often let Humphrey her bear go on show for good causes. So have Princess Anne, Enoch Powell, Derck Nimmo and Lord Bath, whose bear, Clarence, wears spectacles ...

Ted Garnell, *Sunday Express*

If you're sick or lonely in a hospital bed, love IS a Teddy Bear.

Jim Owenby

The feverish collection of Teddy Bears was fanned by the lavish British television production of *Brideshead Revisited* based on Evelyn Waugh's book.

When actor Anthony Andrews appeared as Sebastian Flyte, lovingly hugging the furry Aloysius, nostalgia seemed ratified by the cultural establishment. Devotees have always known that every proper teddy has a mind of its own. Few, though, venture to make the case so directly as Flyte, who orders a silver brush with very stiff bristles – not for grooming, 'but to threaten him with a spanking when he is sulky.'

The Toronto Star

Teddy Bears are an important part of a kid's growing up, a security item. Sometimes mommies and daddies are too busy to listen. Teddy Bears are never too busy.

Andrew Morton, *Time* magazine

Take my dolls
Pull my hair
Take my dog
I don't care
But never take
My Teddy bear

Anonymous

I like my teddy
bear because I like
cuddling.

Allegra, 6

Mr and Mrs Brown first met Paddington on a railway platform. In fact, that was how he came to have such an unusual name for a bear, for Paddington was the name of the station.

Michael Bond, *A Bear Called Paddington*

Do you love your Teddy Bear? Do you carry him around with you, talk to him secretly, cuddle him when you're feeling down? Are you 45? Be not ashamed. The day of the arctophile liberation is at hand.

Vicki Mackenzie, *Women's Weekly*, Australia

> For every bear that ever there was
> Will gather there for certain because
> Today's the day the teddy bears have their picnic.

Jimmy Kennedy, 'The Teddy Bears' Picnic'

I've got a good mind not to take Aloysius to Venice. I don't want him to meet a lot of horrid Italian bears and pick up bad habits.

Evelyn Waugh, *Brideshead Revisited*

The Bluebird was travelling at some 365 miles per hour when the vehicle encountered a patch of wet salt. The car went out of control and was airborne for more than a thousand feet during which time it was performing the most extraordinary manoeuvres and finally ended up a total wreck some three-quarters of a mile from where it left the course. I survived with a fractured skull and lying in hospital some four hours later, realized with horror that Mr Woppit was still in the cockpit. An urgent radio message was despatched and Mr Woppit accorded a police escort from the Flats to the hospital. He was examined on arrival but was found to have survived with nothing worse than a nose out of joint.

Donald Campbell

Poor Teddy Bear is awful bad, he tore his head today,
Its baby's fault, but then I think boys are rough when they play.
Nurse got her needle and some silk, and sewed the hole up quick,
But when the sawdust tumbled out, I cried till I was sick ...

The doctor came at half past five and ordered him to bed,
The doctor's only Daddy but he took Ted's pulse and said,
'This Teddy's awful bad, he must lie very still
And be extremely careful, please he does not catch a chill.'
I scuttled Teddy into bed, and fetched my rocking chair,
And now I'm sitting singing to my poor wee Teddy Bear.

Daisy McGeogh, *The Sick Teddy Bear*

The teddy has physical qualities which make an immediate, unselfish
appeal. One knows instinctively that they are there to help and woe
betide the person, of whatever age, suddenly deprived of their services.

Peter Bull, *Bear With Me*

His love and devotion never fail you. He's a friend in a dark bedroom made of dark shadows. He's the heart of every home you've ever lived in. He's the one sure thing in a world of uncertainties.

Anonymous

I wish I had a Teddy Bear
To sit upon my knee.
I'd take him with my everywhere,
To cuddle up with me.
I'd scorn young men,
No lover then
My lot in life should share
They all might go to Jericho
If I'd a Teddy Bear

Pelissier's *Follies*, 1909

True enthusiasts say a bear's real value is in the holding. Threadbare remnants from childhood have climbed mountains, accompanied RAF pilots into the Battle of Britain and shared foxholes in Vietnam. Cookery expert George Villiers credited 'Rupert' with saving his family when they escaped from Nazi-occupied Norway. Drifting in the North Sea, the bear waved to a British reconnaissance plane, and convinced the crew that the family was British.

Newsweek

We call him that [Symp] because he was extra sympathetic. We used to hug him whenever we were miserable, when we were in disgrace or the rabbits died or when nobody understood us.

Dodie Smith, *Dear Octopus*

The more a bear has been loved, the more children whose companion he has been, the more venerable and prized he is. He becomes like an elderly relative of the household rather than being an object of childhood memories. He is a constant link in a chain of love, his position and status similar to that of a pagan household god, protecting successive generations.

Genevieve and Gerard Picot, *Teddy Bears*

To the extent of not having a Teddy Bear, my early childhood might be described as disadvantaged.

Richard Nixon

Growing up without a Teddy Bear is like missing an important link in the chain of events that make up a lifetime.

Shelley Juchartz

I like teddies because they make you happy.

Louise, 6

Bear, Bear, don't go away
To come again some other day
I will love you if you stay
I will love you anyway.

Traditional

What is it about the Teddy Bear which gives it this fantastic appeal?
This is without doubt one of the most interesting psychological
questions about the history of toys.

Lady Antonia Fraser

Paddington's strength is that he's like the small man
up against life's problems.

Michael Bond

I like teddy bears because they are cuddly and stuffing makes
them cuddle.

Keir, 6

A row of teddy bears sitting in a toyshop, all one size, all one price. Yet
how different each is from the next. Some look gay, some look sad.
Some look standoffish, some look lovable. And one in particular, that
one over there, has a specially endearing expression.
Yes, that is the one we would like please.

Christopher Milne, *The Enchanted Places*

Tom's Teddy was pulled through the window and thrown into a sack. Tom tried to hold on, but he slipped down a massive arm, swung on a big iron key and slithered down a mighty leg. The Teddy Robber was a GIANT!

Ian Beck, *The Teddy Robber*

There is always something regal about a Teddy Bear: no matter how we treat our toy, he has his own dignity, his own secret life.

Rosalie Upton

These jolly little Teddy Bears
Who always love to play,
When hugged by little boys and girls
They'll scare all gloom away.

Anonymous

No other animal has ever achieved quite the same status in toyland. True, there has been the odd lion and tiger, not to mention rabbits, hedgehogs and many others, but none has enjoyed anything like the enduring popularity of the teddy bear, nor have they given rise to quite so many stories: tales of love and kindness, steadfastness, honour and bravery, good manners and thought for others. In short, all the qualities which, deep down, we know to be good and wish we had ourselves.

Michael Bond

Bears mean escapism, whimsy, and fun
– and nobody's too old for that.

Elena Diaz

Please bring my teddy bear to the station. I've had a rough day.

Cartoon, *Wall Street Journal*

Collecting bears is a most enjoyable pastime. It appeals to the hunting instinct (without cruelty).

Colonel Robert Henderson

Bears are not just soft-toy animals; they are best friends and secret-keepers.

Carolyn V. Hall

Teddies are yummy. Not the eat kind of yummy. The love kind.

Cole, 5

The teddy bear plays a great part in the psychological development of people of all ages over the world. This is because he is a truly international figure that is non-religious and yet is universally recognized as a symbol of love and affection. He represents friendship. He functions as a leavening influence amid the trials and tribulations of life.

Colonel Robert Henderson, *Bear Tracks*

For every huntsman's trick
The bear has an escape route.

Old Turkish proverb

When your lover has left and you are lonely in bed, there's a lot to be said for the company of Ted.

Marion Lane

Of all the otherwise mundane objects which stir our collecting instinct ... nothing provokes so much sentiment as the sight of an old battered Teddy Bear.

Carol Ann Stanton

Though it began with youngsters, grown ups are showing a fondness for these plush little toys, with their attractive bodies and quaint features so full of expression. It did not take long for older people to fall under the enchanting spell of teddies and now the wonder is: Where is it all going to end?

Playthings magazine, 1906

Nobody could make Threadbear's squeaker work. Ben's Dad couldn't do it. His mum couldn't do it. Nor could his auntie or his grandma. Nor could any of his friends ...

Mick Inkpen, *Threadbear*

My biggest teddy of them all
Is over four foot seven tall.
He looks most adults in the eye,
And yet he would not hurt a fly.
His name is Arthur Tompkins Bear
And sometimes he's allowed to wear
My father's best black coat and hat
And he looks oh so smart in that.
There isn't room for him in bed.
He guards me from his chair instead.
My very littlest, smallest ted

Is much too wee to come to bed.
He sleeps inside a walnut shell
Which fits around him very well.
He also has it as a boat
And wears a tiny yellow coat.
And these two bears, so large and small,
Are just the greatest friends of all.
Is one too short and one too big?
They really couldn't carc a fig.

Paul Richardson

Teddies make scary things manageable.

Marc Slutsky

Teddy bear, teddy bear turn around,
Teddy bear, teddy bear touch the ground,
Teddy bear, teddy bear go upstairs,
Teddy bear, teddy bear say your prayers.
Teddy bear, teddy bear switch off the light.
Teddy bear, teddy bear say goodnight.

Nursery song

I think about the times during my travels that I've awakened in the night in some strange hotel room, disoriented until I recognized one of my bears sitting nearby, like a sentry. It doesn't matter where I am; if there are teddies nearby, I know that I am safe.

Ted Menton, *The Teddy Bear Lovers' Companion*

The night is long,
But fur is deep.
You will be warm
In winter sleep.

The food is gone
But dreams are sweet
And they will be
Your winter meat.

The cave is dark
But dreams are bright
And they will serve
As winter light.
Sleep, my little cubs, sleep.

Jane Yolen

'What are you thinking about, Teddy Bear?'
'Nothing.'

Aldous Huxley

One of Prince Charles' favourite tunes is 'The Teddy Bears' Picnic', and it is said that on one of his birthdays when he was still at prep school, he requested that the Grenadier Guards play the tune for him and 'Teddy'.

The value of sales of teddy bears in the UK in 1996 was over £45,000,000.

Teddies are very good to make friends with.

Felix, 6

I'm FOUND
and I've someone to play with,
so I'll stay where I am!
decided Small Bear,
and he cuddled up close to the girl
and he stayed ...

Martin Waddell, *Sailor Bear*

Isn't it funny
How a bear likes honey?
Buzz! Buzz! Buzz!
I wonder why he does?

It's a very funny thought that if Bears were bees,
They'd build their nest at the bottom of trees.

A.A. Milne

 76

The secret of the polar bear
Is that he wears long underwear.

Gail Kredenser

To a child, Teddy is a bridge between a human and an animal.
He doesn't mind being taken for a walk, dressed in ridiculous hats,
or even being read to. You can blame him for anything and he won't
deny it. His marvellous face expresses anything a child wants to
feel or hear.

Peter Bull, *A Book of Teddy Bears*

Y is for Yuletide
The grown people's name
For the time when my Teddy
From Santa Claus came.

Anonymous

I am a firm believer in the power of the Teddy Bear. Teddies can be rather like father figures to both young and old. To children in particular they represent goodness, benevolence and kindliness. In my opinion, any parent who attempts to replace this cosy, unharmful toy is a menace!

Dr Joshua Bierer

Algy met a bear
A bear met Algy
The bear was bulgy,
The bulge was Algy.

Anonymous

A teddy bear can be nice and soft to hug, the kind of bear that is required to be able safely to fall asleep.

Erik Ronne

The three bears looked around the room. Father Bear looked at his very big chair.

'Someone has been sitting in my chair,' he said in a very loud voice.

And Mother Bear looked at her medium-sized chair, and in a kindly, medium-sized voice, said, 'Someone has been sitting in my chair.'

And then, there was a squeal from the corner.

'Someone has been sitting in my chair,' said Baby Bear, his face crumpled with dismay, 'and it's all broken!'

The three bears could do little but look at one another, shaking their big bear heads.

'To bed,' said Father Bear. And they did ...

Goldilocks and the Three Bears

Teddy had been Jessica's special bear for as long as he could remember. (Of course that wasn't so very long, because Teddy was a very young bear.)

Dana Kubick, *Midnight Teddies*

But the bear, being very eager to see the royal palace, soon came back again, and peering into the nest, saw five or six young birds lying at the bottom of it.

'What nonsense!' said Bruin, 'this is not a royal palace: I never saw such a filthy place in my life, and you are not royal children, you little base-born brats!'

The Tom-Tit and the Bear

No Teddy bear lover would ever refer to their little furry friend as 'it'. For as a number of psychologists have observed, the teddy is a curious asexual creature, and the choice of whether it be male or female is very much at the discretion of the owner.

Nursery World

A Teddy Bear is soft and warm and inevitably becomes the father figure in the nursery. As people grow older and have to face worries, the teddy becomes the means of recapturing the serenity of childhood.

Carl Bruin

Teddy Bears are the only people I know who are good at turning a blind eye.

Katie Bird

When I was about 20 my mother actually dared send him to the local jumble sale – so I naturally stormed down there and brought him back. You can't fool around with friends like bears.

Jay Heale

Acknowledgements: The Publishers wish to thank everyone who gave permission to reproduce the quotes in this book. Every effort has been made to contact the copyright holders, but in the event that an oversight has occurred, the publishers would be delighted to rectify any omissions in future editions of this book. Children's quotes printed courtesy of Herne Hill School; 'Summoned by Bells', John Betjeman, reprinted courtesy of John Murray Publishers Limited; *Book of Teddy Bears* and *Bear with Me*, Peter Bull, reprinted by permission of Enid Irving and E.P. Dutton; Michael Bond, quoted in *Bear Land* by Deborah Stratton, reprinted courtesy of Michael O'Mara Books; *The Teddy Bear Lovers' Catalogue*, Ted Menton, reprinted courtesy of Ebury Press; *Threadbear*, Mick Inkpen, HarperCollins Publishers; *Midnight Teddies*, Dana Kubrick, published by Walker Books; *I Want My Teddy*, Jez Alborough, published by Walker Books; *A Bear Called Paddington*, Michael Bond, published by HarperCollins Publishers; *The Sunday Express*, extracts reprinted courtesy of Express Newspapers Group; *Sailor Bear*, Martin Waddell, published by Walker Books; *The Teddy Robber*, Ian Beck, Walker Books; *Winnie-the-Pooh* and other titles, A.A. Milne, reprinted courtesy of Methuen Children's Books and E.P. Dutton; *The Enchanted Places*, Christopher Milne, reprinted courtesy of Methuen Children's Books and E.P. Dutton; *Teddy Bears*, Geneviève and Gérard Picot, reprinted courtesy of Weidenfeld and Nicolson; *A Teddy Bear Lover's Book*, Philippa and Peter Waring, extracts reprinted courtesy of Souvenir Press; *Brideshead Revisited*, Evelyn Waugh, reprinted courtesy of Hulton Management and Peters, Fraser and Dunlop; 'Teddy Bear's Picnic' © 1907, M. Whitmark and Sons, USA.